# Charts and Graphs

## Heather C. Hudak
## and James Duplacey

**Weigl**

CALGARY
www.weigl.com

Published by Weigl Educational Publishers Limited
6325 10 Street SE
Calgary, Alberta
T2H 2Z9

Website: www.weigl.com

All of the Internet URLs given in the book were valid at the time of publication. However, due to the dynamic nature of the Internet, some addresses may have changed, or sites may have ceased to exist since publication. While the author and publisher regret any inconvenience this may cause readers, no responsibility for any such changes can be accepted by either the author or the publisher.

Library and Archives Canada Cataloguing in Publication data available upon request.
Fax (403) 233-7769 for the attention of the Publishing Records department.

ISBN 978-1-55388-448-4 (hard cover)
ISBN 978-1-55388-449-1 (soft cover)

Printed in the United States of America
1 2 3 4 5 6 7 8 9 0  12 11 10 09 08

**Editor:** Blaine Wiseman
**Design:** Terry Paulhus

**Photograph Credits:**
Every reasonable effort has been made to trace ownership and to obtain permission to reprint copyright material. The publishers would be pleased to have any errors or omissions brought to their attention so that they may be corrected in subsequent printings.

Getty Images: Pages 3, 5, 10, 11, 13, 17, 21.

We gratefully acknowledge the financial support of the Government of Canada through the Book Publishing Industry Development Program (BPIDP) for our publishing activities.

# Table of Contents

# Learning about Charts and Graphs

Charts and graphs are **graphic organizers**. They both show information in a visual way. Charts and graphs use drawings or tables to compare quantities. Often, they make the information being compared easier to read. Most show the relationship between two or more changing items or **variables**. Charts and graphs differ in the way they display or show information.

**Comparing Countries**

|  | Brazil | Canada | Russian Federation |
|---|---|---|---|
| Population | 186,771,000 | 33,098,932 | 143,420,000 |
| Area | 8,514,877 sq km* | 9,984,670 sq km | 17,075,400 sq km |
| Forest | 5.44 million sq km | 3.10 million sq km | 8.52 million sq km |

* sq km = square kilometres

*Charts often use boxes placed in columns and rows. They show how items in one column or box relate to the items in another. Charts sometimes use words and different colours to help present the **data**.*

**Comparing Forest Area**

| | | |
|---|---|---|
| Brazil | | 3.10 |
| Canada | | 5.44 |
| Russian Federation | | 8.52 |

*Graphs often use images, lines, or bars to show information. A bar graph uses horizontal or vertical bars to plot the information. The length of each bar represents the value of the information being compared.*

# Is it a Chart or a Graph?

Look at the following examples. Which are charts? Which are graphs?
How are they different? How are they similar?

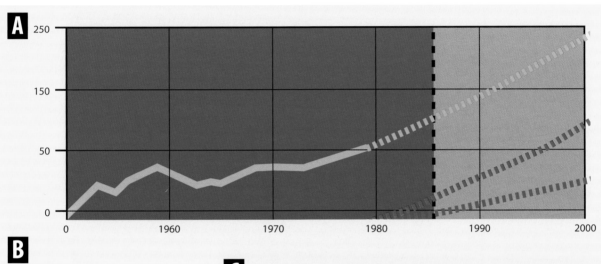

**A**

**B**

**C** **FAUNA AND FLORA IN CANADA**

| | Known species | Estimated total |
|---|---|---|
| **Arachnids** | 3,275 | 11,005 |
| **Birds** | 426 | 426 |
| **Crustaceans** | 3,139 | 4,539 |
| **Fish** | 1,100 | 1,613 |
| **Fungi** | 11,800 | 15,600 |
| **Insects** | 18,530 | 30,330 |
| **Mammals** | 194 | 194 |
| **Plants** | 4,934 | 5,069 |
| **Reptiles** | 42 | 42 |

Fish

Plants

**D** **NUMBER OF ENDANGERED ANIMAL SPECIES**

| | Canada | United States | China |
|---|---|---|---|
| Birds | 27 | 76 | 17 |
| Fishes | 34 | 74 | 21 |
| Mammals | 8 | 15 | 24 |
| Molluscs | 16 | 54 | 0 |
| Reptiles | 12 | 13 | 19 |

*Answers: A) graph B) graph C) chart D) chart*

# Recognizing a Chart

Charts use visual cues, such as words and pictures, to show information. Some charts are large and can be displayed on a wall. Others are small and can be found on the page of a book. Charts may use bright colours or different shapes and symbols to help the reader understand the information that is presented.

*Look at the chart on this page. It shows how different types of **cetaceans** are grouped. The top of the chart shows the group that these animals all belong to. The group is divided into two main types—toothed whales and **baleen** whales. The remaining boxes show which whales, dolphins, and porpoises belong to each of these two types.*

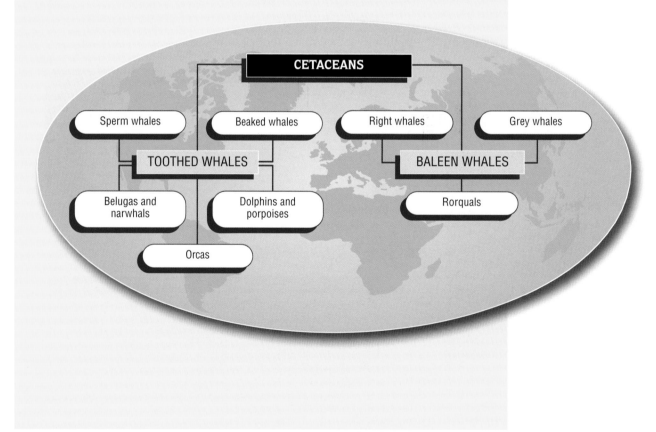

# Reading a Chart

Charts are easy to read. They may use symbols to help you understand the information that is being shown.

Some charts have a legend to show what each symbol means. By looking at the legend and the columns or symbols on the chart, you can learn what information the chart is presenting.

Find all the symbols on this chart. Then, go to the legend to find out what each symbol means. Do the symbols help you understand the chart?

## THE PROCESS FOR BUYING A SHIRT

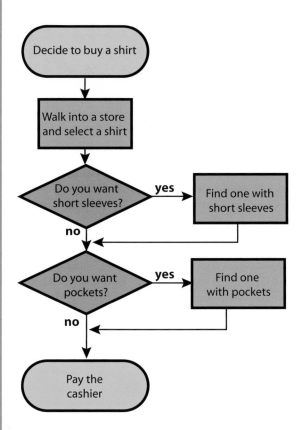

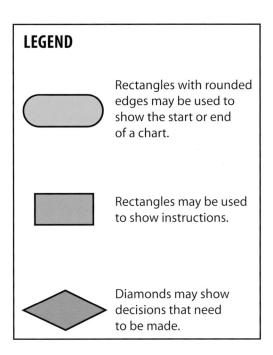

**LEGEND**

Rectangles with rounded edges may be used to show the start or end of a chart.

Rectangles may be used to show instructions.

Diamonds may show decisions that need to be made.

# Knowing Types of Charts

### Flow Charts

Flow charts show the order of events or steps in a process. They also show how the steps work in relation to each other. Flow charts use special symbols to show the steps in the process. Squares, circles, diamonds, and rectangles are common symbols. Arrows often show the connection between items on the chart. A flow chart might show the order for writing a book report.

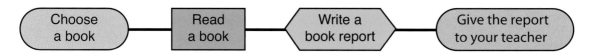

### Pie Charts

Pie charts are shaped like a circle or a pie. The pie has lines, or "slices," to show the different types of information that are being presented. The circle is cut into pieces of different sizes. Each piece is a percentage of the whole. When added together, the total equals 100 percent. A pie chart might show how much of the world's water is drinkable fresh water.

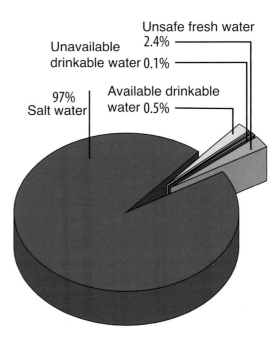

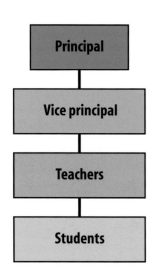

### Organizational Charts

Organizational charts show who is in charge of each section or department within a company or organization. An organizational chart for your school would show the principal at the top. Below the principal would be the vice principal, the teachers, and the students.

# Identifying the Chart

There are three different kinds of charts printed below. Can you identify them? Which one is a pie chart? Which one is a flow chart? Which one is an organizational chart?

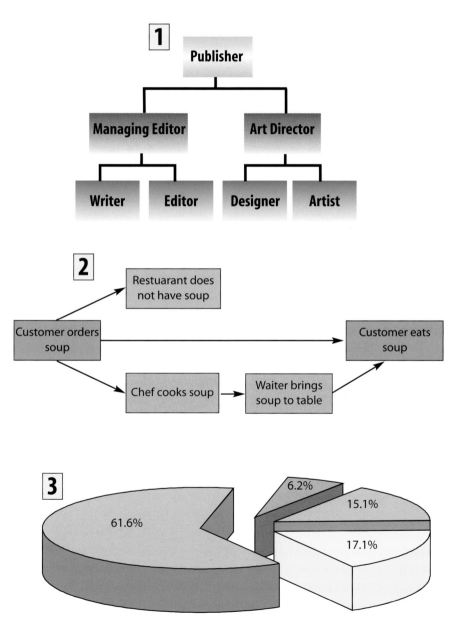

**1**

Publisher

Managing Editor

Art Director

Writer

Editor

Designer

Artist

**2**

Restuarant does not have soup

Customer orders soup

Customer eats soup

Chef cooks soup

Waiter brings soup to table

**3**

61.6%

6.2%

15.1%

17.1%

*Answers: 1) organizational chart 2) flow chart 3) pie chart*

# Using Charts

Charts are used to show information in a clear and accurate way. Similar types of data can be grouped together in rows or in columns. Rows and columns can be colour-coded to show that they contain information that is related. Charts can be used to attract and hold attention, develop an idea, present information to small groups, highlight key points or ideas, and review and preview material.

| PLANET FEATURES | | | | | |
|---|---|---|---|---|---|
| PLANETS | Distance from the Sun | Days to Orbit the Sun | Diameter | Length of Day | Average Temperature |
| Mercury | 58 million km | 88 | 4,879 km | 4,223 hours | 167°C |
| Venus | 108 million km | 225 | 12,104 km | 2,802 hours | 464°C |
| Earth | 150 million km | 365 | 12,756 km | 24 hours | 15°C |
| Mars | 228 million km | 687 | 6,975 km | 25 hours | −63°C |
| Jupiter | 779 million km | 4,331 | 142,984 km | 10 hours | −145°C |
| Saturn | 1,434 million km | 10,747 | 120,536 km | 11 hours | −176°C |
| Uranus | 2,873 million km | 30,589 | 51,117 km | 17 hours | −215°C |
| Neptune | 4,495 million km | 59,800 | 49,527 km | 16 hours | −215°C |

SOCIAL STUDIES ESSENTIAL SKILLS

# Making a Chart

Make a chart to list your favourite types of books and the number of each type you have read. First, make a list of your favourite books. Then, divide the books into categories, such as fiction, science fiction, non-fiction, and biographies. Make a chart using the information you have gathered. Use a different colour for each category.

# Other Types of Charts

## Venn Diagrams

Venn diagrams are made up of two or more overlapping or connecting circles. They are often used to show relationships between sets of things.

The outer circles of a Venn diagram contain different information. The inner circle contains information that is common to all circles. One circle might show animals that live in water. Another circle might show animals that live on land. The inner circle, where the other circles overlap, would show animals that live on land and in water.

| WATER ANIMALS | ANIMALS | LAND ANIMALS |
|---|---|---|
| Dolphins | Sea Lions | Grizzly Bears |
| Salmon | Frogs | Dogs |
| Sharks | Polar Bears | Moose |
| Tuna | Otters | Sparrows |
| Whales | Ducks | Squirrels |

## Flip Charts

Flip charts provide information to groups of people in a room or a meeting. Flip charts are a collection of pages that are bound together at the top. The pages are "flipped," or turned over, as they are used. Each page of the chart has a different piece of information, which is written in large letters so everyone in the room can read it.

**Prime Ministers**

John A. Macdonald
Alexander Mackenzie
John Abbott
John Thompson
Mackenzie Bowell

# Making a Venn Diagram

Make your own Venn diagram. First, do some research about two people you admire, such as Prime Minister Stephen Harper and former Prime Minister Paul Martin.

Write the ways these two people are similar and the ways they are different. For example, what universities did they attend? What did they do before they became prime minister? Did they play sports in university? Draw two circles that overlap. Label one circle for each person you admire. In the area where the circles meet, list all the things the two people have in common. Then, write down all the ways they are different in the proper circle. Try to find at least five items to put in each section.

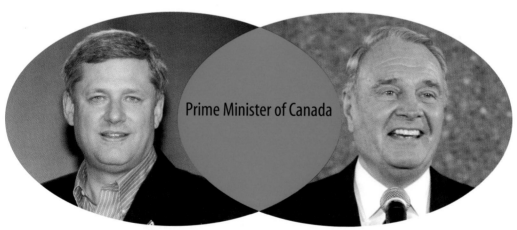

Prime Minister of Canada

| **STEPHEN HARPER** | **PAUL MARTIN** |
| --- | --- |
| Conservative | Liberal |
| Economist | Lawyer |
| University of Calgary | University of Toronto |

# Recognizing a Graph

Graphs are drawings or diagrams that show how numbers or amounts relate to each other. On a graph, numbers are used to show patterns. Many types of graphs have a series of points drawn on a grid. The grid has two **axes**. The x-axis runs horizontally, or from side-to-side, across the graph. The y-axis runs vertically, or from top to bottom. The place where the two axes meet is called the origin. It has a numerical value of zero.

Values are plotted along both the x- and y-axis. Points are marked at different values. Each point has a value on both the x-axis and the y-axis. The place where the point meets on both axes is called the co-ordinate.

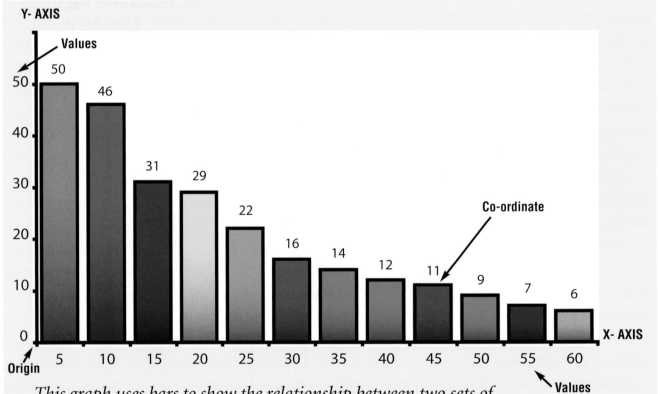

*This graph uses bars to show the relationship between two sets of numbers. According to the graph, which value on the y-axis is equal to 25 on the x-axis?*

# Reading a Graph

This graph shows the relationship between time and people around the world who have had to leave their homes due to war and natural disaster. The x-axis shows the number of people, while the y-axis shows the year.

How many people left their homes in 1981? Run a finger across the grid from the year "1981" on the y-axis until it reaches the end of the bar on the x-axis. Then, run your finger up from the x-axis until it meets the point you found on the y-axis. What is the value of "x?" This is the number of people.

**Displaced People
Due to War or Natural Disaster**

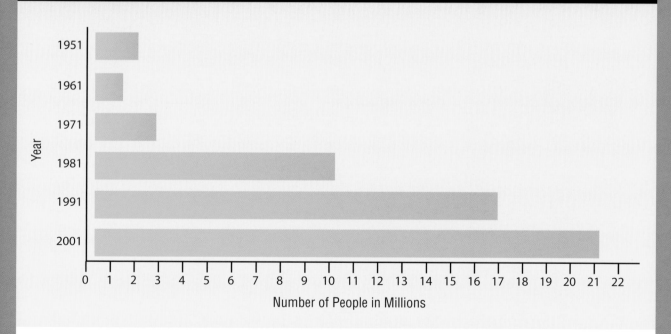

*Answer: About 10 million people left their homes due to war or natural disaster in 1981.*

# Knowing Types of Graphs

There are many types of graphs. Each shows information in a different way.

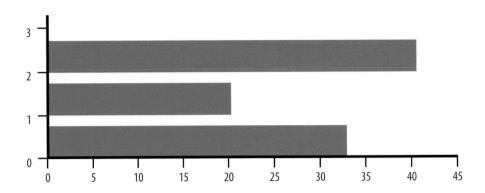

### Bar Graphs

Bar graphs or line graphs are used to compare things. They have vertical or horizontal bars or lines to show information. The larger the value, the taller or longer the bar will be on the graph. A bar or line that has a value of 40 will be twice as tall or long as a bar or line that has a value of 20.

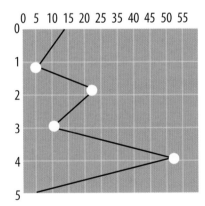

### Scatter Plots

On a scatter plot, dots are placed where the x-axis relates to the y-axis. A line can be drawn between the points to show if the relationship is positive or negative.

### Pictographs

Pictographs use symbols or pictures to compare variables on the axes. For example, stars may be used to show how many students in each grade earned above-average scores on a test.

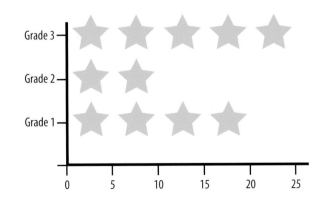

# Identifying the Graph

Look at the graphs on this page. Can you tell which are bar graphs, scatter plots, or pictographs? Do you think the graph is best suited to the data shown? What other type of graph could be used to show the same information?

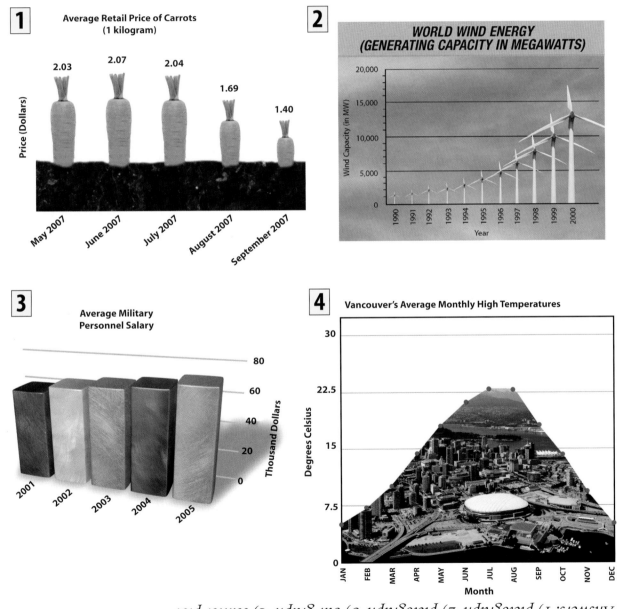

**1** Average Retail Price of Carrots (1 kilogram)

2.03  2.07  2.04  1.69  1.40

Price (Dollars)

May 2007  June 2007  July 2007  August 2007  September 2007

**2** WORLD WIND ENERGY (GENERATING CAPACITY IN MEGAWATTS)

Wind Capacity (in MW)

20,000  15,000  10,000  5,000  0

1990 1991 1992 1993 1994 1995 1996 1997 1998 1999 2000

Year

**3** Average Military Personnel Salary

80  60  40  20  0

Thousand Dollars

2001  2002  2003  2004  2005

**4** Vancouver's Average Monthly High Temperatures

30  22.5  15  7.5  0

Degrees Celsius

JAN FEB MAR APR MAY JUN JUL AUG SEP OCT NOV DEC

Month

*Answers: 1) pictograph 2) pictograph 3) bar graph 4) scatter plot*

# Using Graphs

A graph should be properly labelled. The topic of the variables and the values of the items being compared should be listed on the axes. The graph should be accurate. It should clearly show the correct information and have a title.

If a graph is well made, it will help the reader easily understand the data. A good graph will help explain ideas in a way that is factual and clear. It should be free from extra items. This way, the graph can be read and understood quickly.

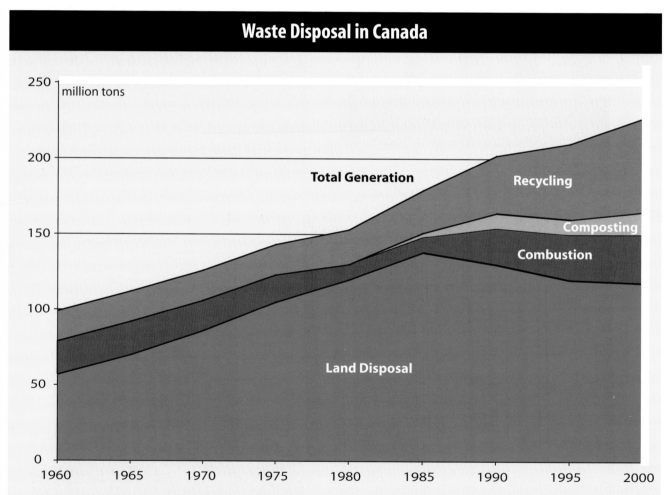

*This graph shows the way waste has been disposed of in Canada over time.*

# Making a Graph

Use the information in this chart to make a graph that compares the distance travelled to the cost of the trip. First, think about which type of graph will best show the information you want to present.

Make a practise graph. You may want to use a different colour for each type of vehicle. Be sure to include a legend showing what the colours represent.

Show the graph to your friends or family. Ask them if they understand the information on the graph. Then, make any corrections or changes that are needed, and draw your final graph.

## TAKE THE TRAIN

For short trips between cities, taking the train can be faster and cheaper than driving, or even flying.

The chart below compares the cost and travel time of three trips by train, car, and plane. Travel time includes the time it takes to get to the station and board the train or plane.

| TRIP | DISTANCE | TRAIN | CAR | PLANE |
|------|----------|-------|-----|-------|
| Moncton to Montreal | 1036 km | Time: 15:55 $128 | Time: 11:30 $100-130 | Time: 4:00 $250 |
| Vancouver to Edmonton | 1244 km | Time: 23:00 $158 | Time: 13:00 $120-150 | Time: 3:30 $100 |
| Saskatoon to Winnipeg | 829 km | Time: 9:00 $88 | Time: 9:00 $100-120 | Time: 3:15 $200 |

# Other Types of Graphs

## Area Graphs

Area graphs can be used to show how something changes over time. Like other graphs, area graphs have an x-axis and a y-axis. Usually, the x-axis has numbers for a time period, and the y-axis has numbers for what is being measured. Area graphs can be used when organizing data that is constantly changing or has been collected in a short time period.

Area graphs often use shaded areas to display their data. This can give the graph a **three-dimensional** look. These graphs sometimes use a legend to explain what each shaded area represents.

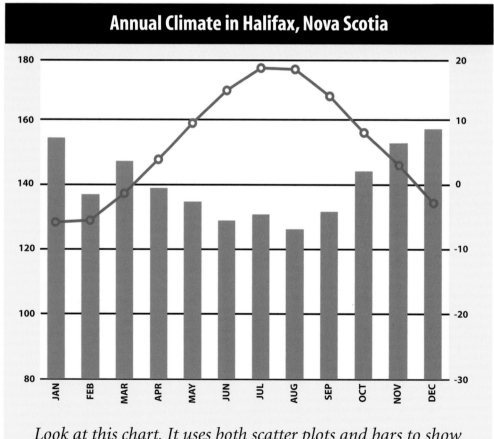

*Look at this chart. It uses both scatter plots and bars to show different kinds of information on one area graph.*

# Making an Area Graph

Make your own area graph. Begin by making a chart called "Pets My Classmates Have." Ask your classmates what kinds of pets they have. Then, write down the types of pets and the number each of your classmates has. Add up the total for each type of pet.

Next, make a graph. Along the x-axis, list the types of pets, such as dogs, cats, and rabbits. Write the numbers 1 through 8 on the y-axis. Then, make an area graph that shows how the types of pets compare to the total for each type. Shade in the area below the lines you have drawn on the graph.

Birds

Cat

Dog

Fish

# Put Your Knowledge to Use

Now that you know how to use charts and graphs, you can create your own. Begin by making a survey for your friends and family. First, select a topic you would like to know more about. Then, form a question about your topic. Think of five possible answers to your question. Ask your friends which one of the five answers they think best answers the question.

Once you have the answers to your questions, create a chart. In one column, write the possible answers. Along the top, write the numbers "0" through "5". Then, put the number of times people selected each answer in the correct column. Now, make a graph using your answers. The following is an example.

| What food would you like to have served in the cafeteria at lunch? | | | | | | |
|---|---|---|---|---|---|---|
| **Votes** | **0** | **1** | **2** | **3** | **4** | **5** |
| **Yogurt** | X | | | | | |
| **Pizzas** | | | | X | | |
| **Salad** | | | X | | | |
| **Lasagna** | | | | | | X |
| **Sub sandwiches** | | X | | | | |

# Websites for Further Research

Many books and websites provide information on charts and graphs. To learn more about charts and graphs, borrow books from the library, or surf the Internet.

To learn more about creating graphs, visit
**http://nces.ed.gov/nceskids/createagraph**

To find out more about charts and graphs, go to
**http://42explore.com/graphs.htm**

To learn how to read charts and graphs, visit
**www.tv411.org/index.shtml**.
Click on "Reading," and then on "Reading Charts and Graphs."

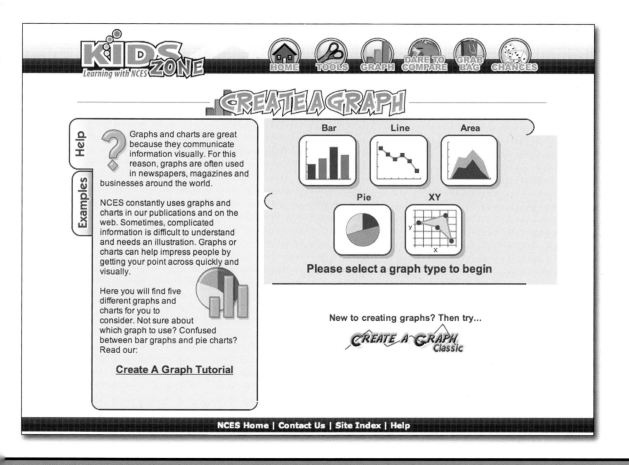

# Glossary

**axes:** two reference lines that measure coordinates

**baleen:** an elastic, hornlike substance grown from the roof of the mouth of some whales

**cetaceans:** a group of marine mammals that have a horizontal tail fin and a blowhole for breathing

**data:** facts collected together for reference

**graphic organizers:** visual representations of information

**three-dimensional:** showing width, depth, and height

**variables:** uncertainties

# Index